For the Teacher

This reproducible study guide consists of lessons to use in conjunction with a specific novel. Written in chapter-by-chapter format, the guide contains a synopsis, pre-reading activities, vocabulary and comprehension exercises, as well as extension activities to be used as follow-up to the novel.

NOVEL-TIES are either for whole class instruction using a single title or for group instruction where each group uses a different novel appropriate to its reading level. Depending upon the amount of time allotted to it in the classroom, each novel, with its guide and accompanying lessons, may be completed in two to four weeks.

The first step in using NOVEL-TIES is to distribute to each student a copy of the novel and a folder containing all of the duplicated worksheets. Begin instruction by selecting several pre-reading activities in order to set the stage for the reading ahead. Vocabulary exercises for each chapter always precede the reading so that new words will be reinforced in the context of the book. Use the questions on the chapter worksheets for class discussion or as written exercises.

The benefits of using NOVEL-TIES are numerous. Students read good literature in the original, rather than in abridged or edited form. The good reading habits, formed by practice in focusing on interpretive comprehension and literary techniques, will be transferred to the books students read independently. Passive readers become active, avid readers.

Novel-Ties® are printed on recycled paper.

SYNOPSIS

This play is set in Salem, Massachusetts in the year 1692. Reverend Samuel Parris is distraught because his daughter Betty has been unconscious for hours. The night before, he discovered Betty, his orphaned niece Abigail, his slave Tituba, and several girls dancing in the forest. Convinced that this unholy behavior would lead to accusations of witchcraft, he has sent for the Reverend Hale, an expert on the subject.

The Putnams, a vindictive couple, disclose that their daughter Ruth is also in a trance. Betty has two other visitors, the Putnams' servant Mercy Lewis and Mary Warren, who has replaced Abigail as servant to the Proctors. Left alone, the girls reveal that Tituba tried to conjure Ruth's dead sisters and Abigail drank blood to conjure the death of Elizabeth Proctor.

When John Proctor arrives, Abigail admits that nothing is wrong with Betty other than fright at being caught dancing in the woods. Abigail, with whom Proctor has had an affair, expresses her love for him, but he spurns her. Betty's sudden screams bring Parris, the Putnams, and two older citizens, Giles Corey and the saintly Rebecca Nurse. The Putnams resent the fact that Rebecca has never lost a child while they have lost seven. It is also obvious that Putnam has had quarrels over property rights with Proctor, Corey, and Rebecca's husband, Francis Nurse.

Reverend Hale arrives and begins interrogating Abigail, who accuses Tituba of calling the Devil. Faced with threats of hanging, the terrified slave confesses and accuses two disreputable old women of witchcraft. Abigail then confesses and starts naming other names, as does Betty.

Eight days later at their home, Proctor and his wife Elizabeth discuss the madness of the witchcraft trials. The atmosphere is tense because Elizabeth cannot forget her husband's affair with Abigail. She urges him to tell the court of Abigail's admission that witchcraft did not cause Betty's condition, but he resists. When Mary Warren enters, she gives Elizabeth a poppet, or rag doll, that she sewed during her hours at court. Mary then discloses that thirty-nine women are now accused of witchcraft and that Elizabeth's name was mentioned. Certain that Abigail wants her dead, Elizabeth again urges Proctor to denounce the girl. When Hale arrives, Proctor tells him about Abigail's lies, but the Reverend is incredulous.

Giles Corey and Francis Nurse arrive to announce the arrest of their wives. Two court officers soon come to Elizabeth, who is accused by Abigail of sending out her spirit to plunge a needle into the girl's belly. After a needle is found in Mary's poppet, Elizabeth is led away in chains. Left alone with Mary, John insists she denounce Abigail.

Proctor brings Mary to court to testify against Abigail. He also produces an affidavit signed by respected people who swear to their good opinions of Elizabeth, Rebecca Nurse, and Martha Corey. Under Judge Hathorne's urgings, Lieutenant Governor Danforth orders the arrest of all the signers. Corey then accuses Putnam of "killing his neighbors for their land," but is himself arrested for contempt when he fails to disclose the name of the man who can substantiate this claim.

When it is time to consider Mary's deposition, Abigail accuses the girl of bewitching her. In desperation, Proctor admits to committing adultery with Abigail, presenting this as a motive for her wanting Elizabeth dead. Danforth calls for Elizabeth to confirm this. She denies it, however, to protect her husband's honor. Elizabeth, now pregnant, is safe from hanging until the birth of the baby. After Elizabeth leaves, Abigail and her followers claim that Mary's spirit is attacking them. Frightened, Mary weakens and joins them, calling Proctor "the Devil's man." Hale, now convinced of the innocence of all the accused, denounces the proceedings.

Act Four opens three months later, a time during which Elizabeth has been imprisoned and Proctor has been tortured and jailed. Word reaches Salem that the citizens of nearby Andover repudiated their witchcraft trials and threw out the court. Parris reveals to Danforth and Hathorne that Abigail and Mercy have fled, taking his life savings. He suggests that the hangings of Rebecca and Proctor be postponed to avoid public anger. Danforth rejects this, but wants Hale to convince them to confess in order to save their own lives. When Hale is unsuccessful, Elizabeth is summoned to plead with her husband, but she refuses to direct his decision. Proctor reluctantly agrees to sign a confession, refusing to implicate others. When told that the confession will be posted, he tears it up. As the play ends, Rebecca and Proctor are escorted out to be hanged.

Mass hysteria (Black Friday! people go crazy)

★1950 Red Scare

(1692)

literally level - witches metaphorical allegory red scar

BACKGROUND INFORMATION

Salem Witchcraft

(92 witches people died)

(no) go along with it so you don't get singled out.

The belief in witchcraft and its ability to produce evil magic was long held by European Christians. False accusations of witchcraft were often used for unethical purposes. This was the case during the Middle Ages when Joan of Arc was burned as a witch by her enemies. In the seventeenth century, James I of England punished hundreds of accused witches in his native Scotland, many of whom were by no coincidence his political enemies. The Puritans in colonial America, because of their literal acceptance of the contents of the Bible, were one group who readily accepted the idea of witches.

Salem was one of various communities established by devout English Puritans who settled the Massachusetts Bay Colony in the early seventeenth century. Despite democratic participation, their local government was a theocracy, a government dominated by religious leaders claiming to represent God. The Puritans were a rigid people, intolerant of the beliefs of others and fearful that any joyous activity, such as dancing, was inspired by the Devil.

Problems began in Salem late in 1691 with odd behavior among some of the community's young girls. When it was revealed that the girls had been dabbling in palmistry, witchcraft was said to be the cause. The girls, who were not themselves accused of being witches, began accusing a few disreputable local women of witchcraft. Before long, they and several adults also began accusing some of the more distinguished members of the community. A form of mass hysteria took hold as the witch trials progressed. By the time they ended, some prominent Massachusetts citizens had been accused, hundreds of alleged witches had been arrested, and nineteen people had been hanged.

(meowing nuns)

cats stopped after being

1500 dancing til it died

Fear.

The McCarthy Era

Tanzania - 3 girls laughing / all laughing
★violence get rid of it

By 1950, the United States was involved in a cold war with the Communist nations, particularly Russia. Fear of the Communist threat to the American way of life precipitated the rise to power of Wisconsin Senator Joseph McCarthy, who launched a crusade against internal subversion by charging that many "known Communists" were working in the State Department. He attacked General of the Army George C. Marshall and leveled charges against the Roosevelt and Truman administrations for "treason." Re-elected to the Senate in 1952, McCarthy attacked many of President Eisenhower's appointments and zealously investigated allegations of subversion in the media. These investigations were labeled "witch hunts" by those who remained level-headed in the face of mass hysteria. McCarthy's power came to an end in 1954, when the Senate voted to condemn the senator for certain of his actions.

In the 1950s, *The Crucible* was widely viewed as a social-protest play, attacking the "witch hunt" tactics of the anti-Communist hearings held by the Wisconsin senator. Audiences of that time, well aware of the madness of McCarthyism, found striking relevance in one of the play's notable lines—"is the accuser always holy now?" Arthur Miller, however, draws only the broadest analogy between the witch hunts of 1692 and those of the McCarthy era. The mood of fear and suspicion permeating both was similar, as was the way accusations were hurled at any who dared criticize the proceedings. *The Crucible*, however, has timeless appeal as gripping drama and is as powerful today as it was in the 1950s. Miller did not deny the obvious contemporary relevance of his play, but he insisted that he was concerned with the larger problem of the dangers of mass hysteria.

READ page directions QUIZ! Act 1 Wednesday / Thursday

Abigail Williams 12

play 18 affair wan added for love entertain

GLOSSARY OF WORDS AND PHRASES

Act One

Dionysiac	related to frenzied behavior or orgies; from Dionysus, Greek god of wine
Erasmus	Desiderius Erasmus, a famous Dutch scholar
Goody	archaic title for a married woman, shortened from *goodwife*
incubi	male demons
In nomine Domini Sabaoth sui filique ite ad infernos	Latin for "In the name of the Lord of Hosts and of His Son depart to the depths of Hell"
Inquisition	Roman Catholic tribunal established in the thirteenth century to discover and punish heresy
klatches	gatherings
Luther	Martin Luther, the German leader of the Protestant Reformation
lye	old spelling of *lie*
Mayflower	ship that brought the first Puritans to America in 1620
meeting house	church
Narragansett	Rhode Island town, which was the scene of warfare between colonists and the Narragansett tribe in 1675
New Jerusalem	the new Holy Land, which the Puritans believed they had founded
Quakers	members of a Protestant sect more lenient than the Puritans
reddish work	evil work
Red Hell	reference to Communism
succubi	female demons

Act Two

bring the man to book	call the man to account
common room	combination kitchen, dining room, and family room
cry me out	call out my name in court
familiar	spirit, often in animal form, believed to act as a servant, as to a witch

Gospel	story and teachings of Jesus Christ in New Testament of the Bible
I'd as lief	I'd prefer
Pontius Pilate	Roman procurator who condemned Jesus to be crucified
poppet	rag doll
pray	please
we must look to cause proportionate	we must look for a reason of equal seriousness

Act Three

at the bar	practicing as a lawyer
broke charity	violated a vow of good faith
ipso facto	Latin for "by that very fact"
Lynn	town near Salem
Marblehead	town near Salem
pound	unit of currency in Britain's American colonies
tittle	very small part
what the angel Raphael said to the boy Tobias	reference to the Book of Tobias, which teaches that God will eventually bless those who are faithful, honest, and charitable

Act Four

Andover	town near Salem
belie themselves	show themselves to be false
fearsome	awesome
gibbet	gallows
greatcoats	heavy overcoats
Joshua	Moses' successor as the leader of the Israelites who led his people in the conquest of Canaan
riles him up	angers him

PRE-READING ACTIVITIES AND DISCUSSION QUESTIONS

1. Preview the play by reading the title and the playwright's name and by looking at the illustration on the cover. What do you think the play will be about? Where and when does it take place? Have you read or seen performances of this or any other play by the same playwright?

2. Read the Background Information about Salem witchcraft on page three of this study guide and do some additional research about the Salem witch trials of 1692. Then read "A Note on the Historical Accuracy of This Play" at the beginning of the book. As you read the play, record the ways the playwright remained true to history and the ways in which he took artistic license.

3. Read the Background Information about the McCarthy era on page three of this study guide and do some additional research to learn more about Senator Joseph McCarthy and the anti-Communist hearings which were called "witch hunts" because they unfairly accused and persecuted individuals, as did the Salem witch trials. What might be considered a modern-day witch hunt?

4. Do some research into the everyday life of the Puritans in Salem in 1692. Find out about their religion, their customs, their laws, their clothing, what they did in their leisure time, etc. Can you draw any conclusions about the relationship between the Puritan way of life and the mass hysteria of the witch trials?

5. The play depicts the strength of the power of suggestion when used to intimidate by those in power. What are some examples of the power of suggestion that you have read about or encountered in your daily life? In what ways can the power of suggestion be used in both positive and negative ways?

6. Is there any circumstance under which you might confess to an illegal act that you did not commit? Are you aware of any time in contemporary life when a person or group of people have done so?

7. The Puritans were intolerant of those with a different belief system from theirs, even though they themselves were persecuted while living in England. What are the effects of intolerance on both its practitioners as well as its victims? What are the dangers inherent in intolerance of any kind?

8. **Cooperative Learning Activity:** In small groups, discuss to what extent an individual has a social and moral responsibility to others. What happens when this responsibility conflicts with responsibility to oneself?

9. **Cooperative Learning Activity:** The word *crucible* means "a severe test or trial." Work with a small group of your classmates to consider this word. Draw a word web, such as the one below, with *crucible* at the center. Then fill in the surrounding circles with examples of personal issues that might be considered a crucible. Compare your responses with those of your classmates.

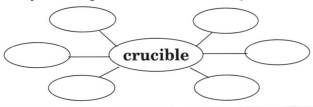

ACT ONE

Vocabulary: Draw a line from each word on the left to its definition on the right. Then use the numbered words to fill in the blanks in each of the sentences below.

1. predilection d   a. dictatorship
2. autocracy a   b. annulment
3. trepidation f   c. attempt to make favorably inclined
4. calumny i   d. preference
5. prodigious j   e. morally loose
6. iniquity g   f. fear
7. inculcation h   g. wickedness
8. abrogation b   h. act of impressing on the mind
9. propitiation c   i. slander
10. licentious e   j. amazing and powerful

· ·

1. Having a fear of flying in an airplane, she approached the upcoming flight with _____.

2. His _____ for debate led to many interesting discussions.

3. Hitler's Germany was a(n) _____.

4. While we consider dancing perfectly tame, to the Puritans it was _____ behavior.

5. The Puritans also believed that the Devil could tempt them to engage in acts of _____.

6. The _____ of the trade agreement would make commerce more difficult between the two countries.

7. The congregation viewed the painting of the crying Madonna as a(n) _____ sign from God.

8. Children may learn prejudice from adults by the _____ of hate.

9. After the argument, the husband's _____ of his wife included the purchase of flowers and an admission that he was wrong.

10. After the newspaper called him a crook, the politician threatened to sue the publisher for _____.

Act One (cont.)

Questions:

1. What is Betty's condition as the play opens? Why can't Dr. Griggs prescribe medicine or special care for her?

2. Why does Reverend Parris ask Abigail to keep Susanna's report about Dr. Grigg's conclusions a secret?

[handwritten: Unconscious - no medical cause, no natural course]
[handwritten: concerned with witchcraft]

3. Why does Reverend Parris worry about revealing what he saw in the forest?

4. What reason does Abigail give Parris for being dismissed from the Proctors' service? What is the real reason of her dismissal?

5. Why does Reverend Parris think he is being coerced to identify witchcraft in his parish? Why doesn't he wish to do this?

6. Why did Ann Putnam send her daughter Ruth to Tituba? What does this suggest about Goody Putnam?

7. How does Proctor treat Abigail after she declares her love for him? Do you think Abigail has reason to believe he still loves her?

8. What quarrels do the Putnams have with the Nurses, the Coreys, and the Proctors? In what way might accusations of witchcraft work in the Putnams' favor?

9. Why is Proctor critical of Reverend Parris?

10. Why is Reverend Hale summoned to Salem? How does he feel about his work?

11. Why does Abigail accuse Tituba of witchcraft? Why does Tituba in turn accuse Goody Good and Goody Osburn of witchcraft?

12. To what do Abigail and Betty confess? What reasons might they have for naming others?

Questions for Discussion:

1. What might be the rational explanations for each of the following strange occurrences:

   - Betty's symptoms—unconscious, then remote and fearful
   - Ruth's illness
   - Death of Mrs. Putnam's babies
   - Giles's inability to read while his wife is reading a questionable book

   Have you ever attributed supernatural causes to an event that turned out to be perfectly natural?

2. Why do you think it is so important for Parris to retain absolute authority over the members of his congregation?

Act One (cont.)

3. Do you think the Reverend Parris' motivation to cooperate with Hale is mainly religious, political, or pragmatic?

4. In what ways do Miller's comments and explanations add to your understanding of the play? If you were in an audience watching the play, would you prefer to have this information read by a narrator or would you be able to appreciate this play without the commentary?

Literary Elements:

I. *Style* — Notice the lengthy commentary that the playwright included in Act One as each historically-based character is introduced. Do you think this text enhances the script or becomes an intrusion? Do you think playgoers experience a diminished play because they lack this historical background? Why do you think Arthur Miller included this text?

II. *Characterization* — Using minimum language and spare action, Miller conveys the complexities and ambiguities of his characters. Consider the following questions in your exploration of these multi-faceted characters:

• Why does Parris fear an investigation into witchcraft?

• Why might Abigail want Betty to remain unconscious?

• How does Abigail's behavior change, depending upon her audience?

• Who should assume guilt in the relationship between Abigail and Proctor?

III. *Setting* — In literature the setting is the time and place in which the story occurs. What is the setting of this play?

_____

How important is the setting to the play?

_____

_____

IV. *Mood* — Mood is the feeling or atmosphere that a writer creates for the reader or audience. Details of settings, actions, language, and imagery all contribute to the mood.

What is the mood of the first act?

_____

What details contribute to this mood?

_____

_____

Act One (cont.)

Literary Device: Irony

Irony refers to a situation that is the opposite of what it seems. Consider the following ironies:

- Why is it ironic that Proctor is the voice of reason against hysteria in the community?
- Why is it ironic that Reverend Parris is particularly concerned with the deed to his house and the terms of his contract?
- Why is it ironic that Abigail and Goody Putnam are the first to accuse others of evil?

Social Studies Connection:

Read the Background Information about the McCarthy era on page three of this study guide and do some additional research to learn why Arthur Miller, in his commentary for Act One, made an analogy between the two opposing camps in Salem and the Communists and Capitalists of the McCarthy era.

Writing Activities:

1. The specific setting of a small, sparse bedroom in the Parris house provides the audience's introduction to Puritan society. In a few well-developed paragraphs, discuss how this setting is an effective background for the action taking place.
2. Imagine you are a member of a Quaker community near Salem. As you visit Salem, write a letter home to one of your acquaintances describing your thoughts and feelings about the events that are taking place.

ACT TWO

Vocabulary: Use a word from the Word Box to replace the underlined word in each of the following sentences. Write the word on the line below the sentence.

WORD BOX				
ameliorate	begrudge	blasphemy	crone	deference
gingerly	ordained	pallor	tainted	theology

1. We observed her <u>paleness</u> and weakness as she tried to stand up after being bedridden for two weeks.

   _____

2. In order to <u>improve</u> a bad situation, you must first devise a plan to change it.

   _____

3. In fairy tales, a witch is often a <u>withered old woman</u>.

   _____

4. Although you are a vegetarian, don't <u>be reluctant to allow</u> me the pleasure of eating a hamburger.

   _____

5. In many Asian countries, old people are treated with <u>courteous respect</u>.

   _____

6. Studying to be a minister, the young man took many courses in <u>religious philosophy</u>.

   _____

7. When he is <u>invested with official authority as a minister</u>, he will return home to serve the poor of his community.

   _____

8. The contents of a dented can might be <u>contaminated</u>.

   _____

9. The new father handled his infant <u>very carefully</u>.

   _____

10. The Puritans believed in swift retribution for even a hint of <u>speech or action showing contempt for God</u>.

    _____

Act Two (cont.)

Questions:

1. How do you know that Proctor has admitted something about his affair with Abigail to his wife Elizabeth?
2. How does Proctor respond when Elizabeth first tells him he must go to court to denounce Abigail? Why does he seem unwilling to expose Abigail?
3. What upsetting news does Mary Warren bring from court?
4. Why doesn't Proctor whip Mary for disobeying him?
5. Why does Hale question Proctor? How does he react to Proctor's responses?
6. Why is Hale incredulous when Proctor tells him that Abigail is lying?
7. What are the charges leveled against Rebecca Nurse and Martha Corey? What do these charges reveal about the proceedings?
8. How does Abigail implicate Elizabeth as a witch? Why does she do this?
9. Why does Proctor call Hale a coward after Elizabeth is arrested?
10. Why does Mary Warren fear testifying against Abigail in court?

Questions for Discussion:

1. Why do you think the author chose to have Proctor's story about his relationship with Abigail told to his wife offstage?
2. Why do you think Sarah Good confessed to witchcraft?
3. To what extent is Hale responsible for what is taking place in Salem? What might he do to stop the madness? Why do you think that he has not done so?
4. How do the witchcraft trials serve the selfish interests of the accusers?
5. Do you think that Mary Warren will expose Abigail?

Literary Devices:

I. *Irony* — What is ironic about Mary Warren's statement that proof of Sarah Good's guilt is "hard proof, hard as rock"?

_____

_____

What is ironic about Proctor's recitation of the commandments?

_____

_____

Act Two (cont.)

II. *Allusion* — Allusion is a reference in literature to a familiar person, place, or event.

   • What is the allusion in the following statement:

   She has an arrow in you yet, John Proctor, and you know it well!

   _____

   What does this allusion reveal about Elizabeth's appraisal of her husband's emotions?

   _____

   _____

   • Why does Proctor allude to Pontius Pilate as he addresses Hale?

   _____

   _____

III. *Metaphor* — A metaphor is a figure of speech in which a comparison of two unlike objects is suggested or implied. For example:

   Theology, sir, is a fortress; no crack in a fortress may be accounted small.

   What is being compared?

   _____

   What does this reveal about Hale's opinion of Proctor?

   _____

   _____

IV. *Stage Directions* — Stage directions are the instructions for the director, performers, and stage crew of a play. Usually set in italics, they are located at the beginning of and throughout a script. They tell the time and place of action and explain how characters move and speak. In what way does Miller use stage directions throughout this act to display the emotions of the characters and to advance the action?

   _____

   _____

Writing Activities:

1. Imagine that you are Elizabeth. In a journal entry, describe how you felt when John first had the affair with Abigail and how you feel now.
2. Write about a time in your own life when being honest caused a conflict.

Act Two (cont.)

Literary Element: Characterization

We learn about characters by what they say and do and by what others say about them. On the chart below, record something John Proctor says, something he does, and something that is said about him. Then next to each example, tell what it reveals about his personality.

John Proctor		
		What Is Revealed
What he says		
What he does		
What others say about him		

ACT THREE

Vocabulary: Word analogies are equations in which the first pair of words has the same relationship as the second pair of words. For example: DOMINANT is to SUBMISSIVE as BOUNTIFUL is to SPARSE. Both pairs of words are opposites. Choose the best word from the Word Box to complete each of the analogies below.

WORD BOX

contentious	deposition	effrontery	guile	immaculate
imperceptible	probity	remorseless	undermine	unperturbed

---

1. CHARITABLE is to MEAGER as REGRETFUL is to _____.

2. ENERGETIC is to VIGOROUS as ARGUMENTATIVE is to _____.

3. REHEARSAL is to PLAY as _____ is to TRIAL.

4. _____ is to STRENGTHEN as PUBLICIZE is to CONCEAL.

5. OBVIOUS is to EVIDENT as _____ is to SUBTLE.

6. OPTIMISM is to PESSIMISM as TIMIDITY is to _____.

7. OPERATING ROOM is to _____ as PIG STY is to FILTHY.

8. _____ is to INTEGRITY as ELATION is to RAPTURE.

9. DECEIT is to _____ as TRUTH is to CANDOR.

10. DISCONSOLATE is to CHEERFUL as TROUBLED is to _____.

Questions:

1. Why does Giles Corey feel guilty for the charges of witchcraft that have been leveled against his wife?

2. Contrast Parris's and Hale's reactions as Proctor, Corey, and Nurse plead their cases before Danforth.

3. Why does Danforth hesitate to accept Mary Warren's statement that her prior testimony was pretense?

4. What will happen to the people who signed the deposition in support of Elizabeth Proctor, Martha Corey, and Rebecca Nurse? What is the significance of Danforth's comment that the people are either with the court or "must be counted against it"?

Act Three (cont.)

5. Why does Corey refuse to divulge the name of the man who can substantiate his claim that Putnam is "killing his neighbors for their land"? What does this suggest about Corey?

6. What accusations does Proctor make against Abigail?

7. What is Elizabeth's response when she is asked whether her husband was unfaithful? Why does she respond this way?

8. What developments have brought about the complete reversal of Hale's attitude toward the witchcraft trials?

9. Why does Mary denounce her deposition and side with Abigail against Proctor?

Questions for Discussion:

1. Why do you think Danforth would have suspended charges against Elizabeth?

2. Why do you think Mary Warren was once able to faint at will but cannot do so upon Danforth's request?

3. Why do you think that Danforth is so quick to believe Abigail? Why is Hale now able to appreciate Abigail's deception?

4. Do you think Mary Warren is a victim, or do you find her as culpable as Abigail and the other girls?

Literary Devices:

I. *Metaphor* — What is being compared in Danforth's metaphor?

> We burn a hot fire here; it melts down all concealment.

_____

What mood and tone does this metaphor create?

_____

_____

What does Proctor compare in the following metaphor?

> I have made a bell of my honor? I have rung the doom of my good name.

_____

Why is this an apt comparison?

_____

_____

Act Three (cont.)

II. *Irony* — Situational irony refers to a contrast between what is expected to happen and what actually happens. Dramatic irony occurs when readers know more about a situation in a story or play than a character does.

What is the situational irony in the actions of the court?

_____

_____

What is the dramatic irony in Elizabeth's response when she is asked why she dismissed Abigail?

_____

_____

Literary Elements:

I. *Conflict* — The plot is the arrangement of a series of incidents that make up the story. A conflict, which is a struggle between opposing forces, creates the story's dramatic tension, moving the plot forward. There are many different kinds of conflict such as conflict between people, conflict with nature, conflict with society, and personal conflict consisting of a mental struggle going on within a character. In the chart below, describe the conflicts in the play.

Person *vs.* Person	
Person *vs.* Society	
Person *vs.* Self	

Act Three (cont.)

II. *Character Development* — In *The Crucible*, character traits are revealed through the characters' reactions to events taking place around them. Use a Venn diagram, such as the one below, to compare and contrast the characters of Hale and Danforth. Consider their reactions to the accusations of witchcraft, the testimony, and the evidence. Record their similarities in the overlapping part of the circles.

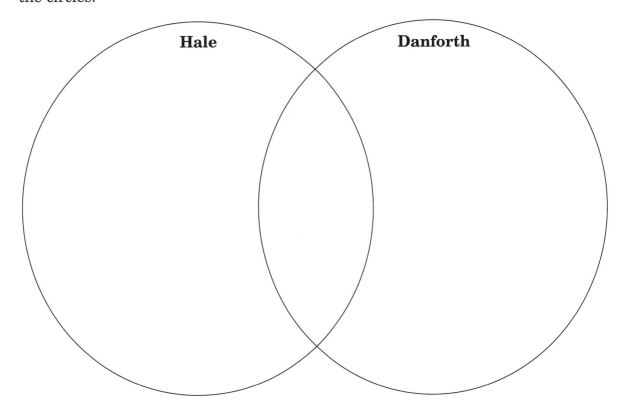

Hale   **Danforth**

Social Studies Connection:

Recall the information you read about the Senator Joseph McCarthy congressional hearings of the 1950s. How would you compare the Salem witch trials at the end of the seventeenth century to the McCarthy hearings? Specifically, how does Danforth's demand that Giles Corey name the man who gave him information parallel similar instances in the McCarthy hearings?

Writing Activities:

Imagine you are a television news reporter who has been present during Danforth's questioning of Proctor, Mary Warren, Abigail, and Elizabeth. Prepare a news presentation for an evening news broadcast to describe, as objectively as possible, what occurred. Then play the role of a news commentator and prepare a report presenting an opinion of the events that occurred.

ACT FOUR

Vocabulary: Use the context to help you choose the best meaning for the underlined word in each of the following sentences. Circle the letter of the answer you choose.

1. Shocked by the awful conditions in the prison, the visitor stood with his mouth <u>agape</u>.
   a. smiling slightly   b. drooling   c. wide open   d. closed tightly

2. After the quarreling nations reached a compromise, a more <u>conciliatory</u> atmosphere prevailed.
   a. civil   b. stubborn   c. belligerent   d. reckless

3. The prisoner was relieved when the governor issued a <u>reprieve</u> just minutes before he was to be executed.
   a. sentence   b. law   c. postponement   d. report

4. If you go against the <u>statutes</u> of your community, you will be punished.
   a. boundaries   b. structures   c. crimes   d. laws

5. Even though I begged my father to let me stay out late, he remained <u>adamant</u> that I respect a midnight curfew.
   a. submissive   b. unyielding   c. anxious   d. fatigued

6. The <u>sibilance</u> of steam escaping from the valve in the old radiator kept me awake all night.
   a. hissing sound   b. deafening roar   c. bad odor   d. bright colors

7. The prisoner was brought to trial after the grand jury issued an <u>indictment</u>.
   a. execution   b. legal accusation   c. legal sentence   d. decree

8. Because the convicted criminal displayed <u>penitence</u>, the judge showed mercy during sentencing.
   a. fear   b. anger   c. remorse   d. calmness

9. The town of Salem was split by <u>factionalism</u>.
   a. harmony   b. group dissension   c. religious   d. group effort
                                                             doctrine

10. Realizing its gross injustice, the congregation <u>rescinded</u> the excommunication of those implicated in witchcraft.
    a. avoided   b. asserted   c. resolved   d. revoked

Act Four (cont.)

Questions:

1. What news does Parris relate to Danforth and Hathorne? How has this news affected Parris?

2. Why does Parris fear a riot in Salem even after Hathorne points out that the executions so far have met with "high satisfaction" in the town? What conditions in Salem does Hale describe that could lead to a riot?

3. Why does Hale want the convicted to confess? How does his motivation differ from that of Danforth and Parris?

4. What argument does Proctor use to convince Elizabeth that he should make a false confession?

5. Why does Elizabeth refuse to advise Proctor on whether or not to confess?

6. How does Rebecca Nurse influence Proctor's decision to confess?

7. Why does Proctor refuse to sign the confession?

8. Why does Elizabeth say "He have [sic] his goodness now. God forbid I take it from him!" as Proctor is led to the gallows?

Questions for Discussion:

1. Do you agree with Hale that it is right to lie in order to protect your own life or the lives of others? Are there any circumstances under which you think it might not be right to lie?

2. Do you think Elizabeth should have tried to convince Proctor to confess, or was she right to let him make his own decision?

3. Do you think Proctor should have torn up his confession?

4. In the end, do you think either Danforth or Parris really believed that the witch trials had merit? Do you think either of these characters reached an awareness of the evil they engendered?

5. Miller states that in the aftermath of the witch trials, "the power of the theocracy in Massachusetts was broken." Do you think that only something as calamitous as the witch trials could have achieved this?

Literary Elements:

I. *Characterization* — How does Proctor's emphasis on the importance of his name relate to his own self-discovery by the end of the play? Trace Proctor's character development through the play, showing how it might be a man's journey into the discovery of himself.

Act Four (cont.)

II. *Resolution* — The resolution is the part of the plot that presents the final outcome. It shows how the main conflict is resolved. What is the resolution of this play? What other outcomes might the play have had? Which resolution do you prefer and why?

Literary Device: Figurative Language

A simile is a figure of speech in which a comparison between two unlike objects is stated directly using the words "like" or "as." In a metaphor, the comparison is suggested or implied. In the following example, Miller makes use of both simile and metaphor:

> I came into this village like a bridegroom to his beloved, bearing gifts of high religion; the very crowns of holy law I brought, and what I touched with my bright confidence, it died; and where I turned the eye of my great faith, blood flowed up.

What is the effect of Hale's simile in which he compares himself to a bridegroom?

_____

_____

What metaphors does Hale use? Do you find them appropriate? Why or why not?

_____

_____

_____

_____

Writing Activities:

1. In a few well developed paragraphs, describe what you think would have happened if Proctor had not torn up his confession. What would the lives of Proctor and Elizabeth have been like? What would have happened to the others accused of witchcraft? How would the citizens of Salem have reacted?

2. Imagine that you are a drama critic who attends the opening of a revival of *The Crucible*. Write a review of the play. You will have to imagine the acting performances and other production details. Also, indicate the ways in which this play speaks to a contemporary audience.

CLOZE ACTIVITY

The following passage has been taken from the author's commentary on Reverend Hale in Act One of the play. Read it through completely and then fill in each blank with a word that makes sense. Afterwards you may compare your language with that of the author.

Mr. Hale is nearing forty, a tight-skinned, eager-eyed intellectual. This is a beloved errand for him; _____[1] being called here to ascertain witchcraft he _____[2] the pride of the specialist whose unique _____[3] has at last been publicly called for. _____[4] almost all men of learning, he spent _____[5] good deal of his time pondering the _____[6] world, especially since he had himself encountered _____[7] witch in his parish not long before. _____[8] woman, however, turned into a mere pest _____[9] his searching scrutiny, and the child she _____[10] allegedly been afflicting recovered her normal behavior _____[11] Hale had given her his kindness and _____[12] few days of rest in his own _____.[13] However, that experience never raised a doubt _____[14] his mind as to the reality of _____[15] underworld or the existence of Lucifer's many-faced _____.[16] And his belief is not to his _____.[17] Better minds than Hale's were—and still _____[18] —convinced that there is a society of _____[19] beyond our ken. One cannot help noting _____[20] one of his lines has never yet _____[21] a laugh in any audience that has _____[22] this play; it is his assurance that "_____[23] cannot look to superstition in this. The _____[24] is precise." Evidently we are not quite _____[25] even now whether diabolism is holy and _____[26] to be scoffed at. And it is no accident that we should be so bemused.

POST-READING ACTIVITIES AND DISCUSSION QUESTIONS

1. Read Act Two, Scene 2, which appears in the appendix. Why do you think that Miller dropped this scene from the play? Do you think it should have been included? Debate this issue with classmates who hold the opposing view.

2. This play about the Salem witch trials had great relevance for audiences of the 1950s who were living through the McCarthy era. Assess the play's relevance today. In what way can a play set in the late 1600s, written in the 1950s, have any bearing on contemporary life?

3. Massachusetts Colony was considered a Puritan theocracy, a form of government in which the controlling force resides in a single religious establishment. What governments in today's world function as theocracies? What attempts have been made since the days of the Puritans to adopt some aspects of a theocracy in America?

4. Do some research to find out how Arthur Miller himself became a victim of McCarthyism. What parallels can you draw between the testimony given at the witch trials in the play and Miller's own testimony before the House Un-American Activities Committee? What was the outcome of Miller's testimony?

5. **Cooperative Learning Activity:** Work with a small group of your classmates to design a program for a new production of *The Crucible*, complete with cover design, a list of the cast, a substantial plot summary, and ads. Cast the play with television or movie actors who you think are suited to the roles.

6. Working with classmates, select a scene from the play that you feel is especially dramatic. Rehearse the scene and then present it to the class. If possible, include appropriate costumes, props, and scenery.

7. What does this play have to say about the frailty of civil liberties? What contemporary issues point this up as did the Salem witch trials of the 1600s? How might today's war on terrorism threaten the civil rights of individuals?

8. What issues in contemporary society reveal how self-seeking individuals may become blind to justice?

9. A tragic hero is usually a high-ranking or respected person whose personality is marred by a fatal weakness, or tragic flaw, that causes his or her downfall. The hero either makes a discovery of past folly or is presented with an agonizing dilemma. To what degree does Proctor fit the mold of the tragic hero?

10. A symbol is a person, a place, an object, or a situation that exists on a literal level within a work but also represents something on a figurative level, usually an abstract quality or range of qualities. What do the witch trials symbolize? What might be symbolized by the characters of Parris, Hale, Danforth, and Proctor?

Post-Reading Activities and Discussion Questions (cont.)

11. The theme in a literary work is its controlling idea. It is the underpinning beneath the plot, the force behind the characterization. In *The Crucible* there is not one single theme, but many themes competing for attention and prominence. Examine the following themes and discuss how each is manifest in the play.

    - commitment and loyalty
    - individual rights *versus* societal authority
    - moral integrity
    - responsibility to others *versus* responsibility to self
    - effects of mass hysteria
    - power of suggestion
    - corrupting power of authority

SUGGESTIONS FOR FURTHER READING

Drama

Ibsen, Henrik Johan. *An Enemy of the People*. Rupert Hart-Davis.
Lawrence, Jerome, and Robert E. Lee. *Inherit the Wind*. Random House.
* Shakespeare, William. *Hamlet*. Penguin.
* _____. *Julius Caesar*. Penguin.

Other Fiction

Forbes, Esther. *A Mirror for Witches*. Dell.
* Golding, William. *Lord of the Flies*. Putnam.
Hawthorne, Nathaniel. *The House of the Seven Gables*. G.K. Hall.
* _____. *The Scarlet Letter*. Random House.
* Kesey, Ken. *One Flew Over the Cuckoo's Nest*. New American Library.
* Orwell, George. *Animal Farm*. New American Library.
* _____. *1984*. New American Library.
Petry, Ann. *Tituba of Salem Village*. HarperCollins.
* Speare, Elizabeth George. *The Witch of Blackbird Pond*. Random House.
* Steinbeck, John. *Of Mice and Men*. Penguin.
* Twain, Mark. *The Adventures of Huckleberry Finn*. Random House.

Nonfiction

Boyer, Paul, and Stephen Nissenbaum. *Salem Possessed*. Cambridge.
Hansen, Chadwick. *Witchcraft at Salem*. Braziller.
Morgan, Edmund S. *Visible Saints: The History of a Puritan Idea*. New York
         University.
Moss, Leonard. *Arthur Miller*. Twayne.

Some Other Plays by Arthur Miller

After the Fall. Penguin
All My Sons. Penguin.
Broken Glass. Penguin.
* *Death of a Salesman*. Penguin.
Incident at Vichy. Penguin.
The Last Yankee. Penguin.
The Price. Penguin.
A View from the Bridge. Penguin.

* NOVEL-TIES Study Guides are available for these titles.

ANSWER KEY

Act One

Vocabulary: 1. d 2. a 3. f 4. i 5. j 6. g 7. h 8. b 9. c 10. e; 1. trepidation 2. predilection 3. autocracy 4. licentious 5. iniquity 6. abrogation 7. prodigious 8. inculcation 9. propitiation 10. calumny

Questions: 1. As the play opens, Betty is lying unconscious. Susanna relates to Reverend Parris that Dr. Griggs could find no medical reason for Betty's condition and thinks that it might have an "unnatural" cause. 2. Reverend Parris does not want Abigail to tell anyone about Susanna's report from Dr. Griggs because many of his parishoners are concerned about witchcraft. 3. Since dancing is forbidden in a Puritan community, and there is a growing fear of witchcraft, the Reverend fears for his own reputation and his daughter's life. He worries that there are people in his congregation who will use this issue to get rid of him. 4. Abigail says that Goody Proctor is a bitter woman who wanted a slave, not a servant. She was actually dismissed for having an affair with John Proctor. 5. Reverend Parris thinks he is being coerced to identify the strange incidents of illness in the community as witchcraft to Thomas Putnam, who threatens that his enemies in the parish will turn against him even more if he doesn't do so. Reverend Parris does not wish to announce witchcraft because of Tituba and Betty's involvement, which could cast dispersion on himself. 6. Ann Putnam sent Ruth to Tituba in order to conjure up her dead sisters. This suggests that Goody Putnam is a superstitious woman who actually cares little for the welfare of her daughter. 7. After she declares her love for him, Proctor spurns Abigail. Answers to the second part of the question will vary, but students might suggest that Proctor's playful manner toward Abigail when he first enters might give her hope that he does care for her. 8. The Putnams have quarreled with the others over property rights, and they resent the fact that Rebecca has never lost a child or grandchild. The accusations of witchcraft against Rebecca could result in her enemies obtaining her land. 9. Proctor is critical of Reverend Parris's hell and brimstone sermons. He resents the authority of the head of the church over his life, wishing for a dialogue that Parris will not permit. 10. Hale is summoned to Salem because he is an intellectual, an expert on witchcraft. He considers himself a doctor who will use scientific principles to ascertain whether the devil is at work in Salem. 11. Abigail accuses Tituba of witchcraft so that she will no longer be the focus of Hale's interrogation. Tituba is an easy target of vilification because of her race and because she seems exotic in a Puritan community. Tituba probably accuses the other women to save her own life since hanging is punishment for witches. 12. Abigail and Betty confess to dancing for the Devil. They probably name others to avoid their own punishment and to get revenge on people they dislike.

Act Two

Vocabulary: 1. pallor 2. ameliorate 3. crone 4. begrudge 5. deference 6. theology 7. ordained 8. tainted 9. gingerly 10. blasphemy

Questions: 1. Because Elizabeth and John seem overly careful and unsure around each other, it becomes evident that Proctor admitted something about his affair. His behavior suggests his feelings of guilt, and Elizabeth's behavior suggests that she cannot fully forgive him. 2. When Elizabeth tells her husband he must denounce Abigail, he responds by saying that he will think about it. Proctor seems unwilling to expose Abigail because he may fear that she will expose him as an adulterer. 3. Mary relates that thirty-nine women have been arrested, Goody Osburn will hang, and Elizabeth's name was mentioned in court. 4. Proctor resists the urge to whip Mary when he realizes she has the power to condemn his wife in court. 5. Hale questions Proctor because of suspicions about his lack of attendance at meeting, the fact that his third son is not baptized, and some unspecified suspicion about his wife Elizabeth. Hale does not seem completely satisfied with Proctor's responses. He recommends that Proctor attend meeting and have his son baptized. 6. Hale refuses to accept Proctor's statement that Abigail lied because many people have confessed to witchcraft, and he doesn't want to

admit that he may be convicting innocent people. 7. Rebecca is charged with the murder of Goody Putnam's babies, and Martha is charged with bewitching a neighbor's pigs with her books. These charges reveal that the proceedings are out of hand, with vindictive neighbors using them to get revenge against imagined wrongs. 8. Abigail, knowing that the poppet Mary made for Elizabeth has a needle in it, says that Elizabeth's spirit pushed a needle into her belly. The motivation for her assertion is her hatred for Elizabeth because she is the impediment to her having Proctor to herself. 9. Proctor calls Hale a coward because he does not speak up against what he must know is injustice. 10. Mary Warren fears testifying against Abigail because she believes Abigail will kill her and implicate Proctor as an adulterer.

Act Three

Vocabulary: 1. remorseless 2. contentious 3. deposition 4. undermine 5. imperceptible 6. effrontery 7. immaculate 8. probity 9. guile 10. unperturbed

Questions: 1. Corey feels guilty because he is the one who asked Hale why his wife read so much. It was then assumed that the books she read concerned witchcraft and she was condemned. 2. Parris warns Danforth not to listen to Proctor, Corey, and Nurse trying to thwart their case. Hale, on the other hand, asks that they be able to plead their case and supports them. 3. If Danforth were to accept Mary Warren's denial, it would make the current court proceedings a sham. His character and reputation rest upon the sanctity of these trials. 4. Those who signed the deposition will be held for questioning by the court. Danforth believes that there is no room for argument or free speech in the court; those who are not in complete agreement with the authorities are automatically regarded as enemies. 5. Corey will not divulge the name of another because he is a responsible man who will not willingly be the cause of another's suffering. 6. Proctor accuses Abigail of being a liar, a whore, and an attempted murderer. 7. Elizabeth denies that her husband was unfaithful. She lies to protect her husband's honor, thus showing she loves him. 8. Hale's attitude changes because he now sees the lack of compassion in Danforth and Hathorne; he perceives the bias of the court which views every defense as an attack on its authority; and he recognizes that Abigail and others are motivated by private vengeance. 9. Mary, being weak, finds it easier to give in to Abigail than to fight her and risk being hanged.

Act Four

Vocabulary: 1. c 2. a 3. c 4. d 5. b 6. a 7. b 8. c 9. b 10. d

Questions: 1. Parris relates the news that Abigail and Mercy Lewis have fled, robbing Parris of all his money, and that the nearby town of Andover has overthrown the court and denounced the witchcraft trials. Parris has become a frightened and broken man. 2. Parris fears a riot because the accused, Rebecca and Proctor, are important citizens of Salem, in contrast to the others who have been executed. Hale describes desperate conditions in Salem that may lead to riot: children have been orphaned and farm animals and crops go unattended. 3. Even though Hale knows the accused are innocent, he wants them to confess in order to save their lives. Danforth and Parris want them to confess to stop a possible riot. 4. Proctor argues that since he is not a good man, nothing is spoiled by lying now. 5. Elizabeth will not advise her husband because she believes he must answer to his conscience alone so that he can find peace with himself. 6. Rebecca's courage to stand by her principles and refuse to confess influence Proctor to remain firm in his refusal to confess. 7. Proctor refuses to sign the confession because he asserts that he has given the court his soul, but wants them to leave him his name. He has given the court his soul by lying, but he wants his good name so that he can live with himself and so that his children will be able to look up to him. He also refuses to allow Danforth and his cohorts to benefit from his signed confession. 8. When Elizabeth says, "He have his goodness now. God forbid I take it from him!"she means that Proctor is at peace with himself for listening to his conscience and she will not disturb this peace.